What's My Style?

I love creating elaborate patterns packed with detail so I can do lots of intricate coloring. I try to use as many colors as possible. Then I layer on lots of fun details. Here are some more examples of my work.

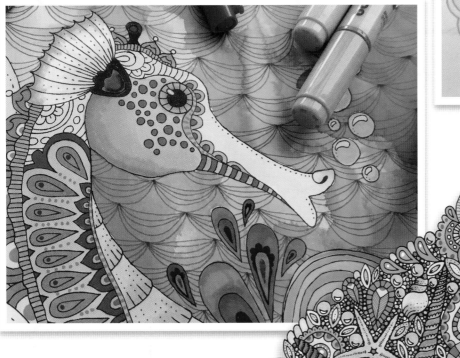

My studio is filled with natural light, tons of coloring supplies, and lots of inspiration, all of which motivate me to create and color!

Where to Start

You might find putting color on a fresh page stressful. It's okay! Here are a few tricks I use to get the ink flowing.

Start with an easy decision. If a design has leaves, without a doubt, that's where I start. No matter how wacky and colorful everything else gets, I always color the leaves in my illustrations green. I have no reason for it; it's just how it is! Try to find something in the design to help ground you by making an easy color decision: leaves are green, the sky is blue, etc.

Get inspired. Take a good look at everything in the illustration. You chose to color it for a reason. One little piece that you love will jump out and say, "Color me! Use red, please!" Or maybe it will say blue, or pink, or green. Just relax—it will let you know.

Follow your instincts. What colors do you love? Are you a big fan of purple? Or maybe yellow is your favorite. If you love it, use it!

Just go for it. Close your eyes, pick up a color, point to a spot on the illustration, and start! Sometimes starting is the hardest part, but it's the fastest way to finish!

Helpful Hints

There is no right or wrong. All colors work together, so don't be scared to mix it up. The results can be surprising!

Try it. Test your chosen colors on scrap paper before you start coloring your design. You can also test blending techniques and how to use different shapes and patterns for detail work—you can see how different media will blend with or show up on top of your chosen colors. I even use the paper to clean my markers or pens if necessary.

Make a color chart. A color chart is like a test paper for every single color you have! It provides a more accurate way to choose colors than selecting them based on the color of the marker's cap. To make a color chart, color a swatch with each marker, colored pencil, gel pen, etc. Label each swatch with the name or number of the marker so you can easily find it later.

Do you like warm colors?

How about cool colors?

Maybe you like warm and cool colors together!

Keep going. Even if you think you've ruined a piece, work through it. I go through the same cycle with my coloring: I love a piece at the beginning, and by the halfway point I nearly always dislike it. Sometimes by the end I love it again, and sometimes I don't, and that's okay. It's important to remember that you're coloring for you— no one else. If you really don't like a piece at the end, stash it away and remember that you learned something. You know what not to do next time. My studio drawers are full of everything from duds to masterpieces!

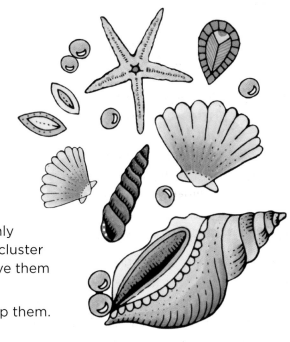

Be patient. Let markers, gel pens, and paints dry thoroughly between each layer. There's nothing worse than smudging a cluster of freshly inked dots across the page with your hand. Just give them a minute to dry and then you can move on to the next layer.

Use caution. Juicy/inky markers can "spit" when you uncap them. Open them away from your art piece.

Work from light to dark. It's much easier to make something darker gradually than to lighten it.

Shade with gray. A mid-tone lavender-gray marker is perfect for adding shadows to your artwork, giving it depth and making it pop right off the page!

Try blending fluid. If you like working with alcohol-based markers, a refillable bottle of blending fluid or a blending pen is a great investment. Aside from enabling you to easily blend colors together, it can help clean up unwanted splatters or mistakes—it may not take some colors away completely, but it will certainly lighten them. I use it to clean the body of my markers as I'm constantly smudging them with inky fingers. When a marker is running out of ink, I find adding a few drops of blending fluid to the ink barrel will make it last a bit longer.

Layering and Blending

I love layering and blending colors. It's a great way to create shading and give your finished piece lots of depth and dimension. The trick is to work from the lightest color to the darkest and then go over everything again with the lightest shade to keep the color smooth and bring all the layers together.

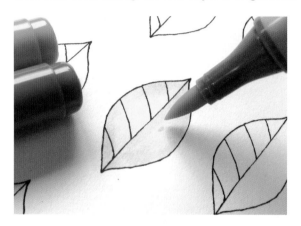

1 Apply a base layer with the lightest color.

2 Add the middle color, using it to create shading.

3 Smooth out the color by going over everything with the lightest color.

4 Add the darkest color, giving your shading even more depth. Use the middle color to go over the same area you colored in Step 2.

5 Go over everything with the lightest color as you did in Step 3.

Patterning and Details

Layering and blending will give your coloring depth and dimension. Adding patterning and details will really bring it to life. If you're not convinced, try adding a few details to one of your colored pieces with a white gel pen—that baby will make magic happen! Have fun adding all of the dots, doodles, and swirls you can imagine.

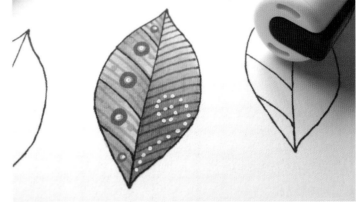

1 Once you've finished your coloring, blending, and layering, go back and add simple patterning like lines or dots. You can add your patterns in black or color. For this leaf, I used two different shades of green pen.

2 Now it's time to add some fun details using paint pens or gel pens. Here I used white, yellow, and more green.

This design really pops with lots of patterning and little details.

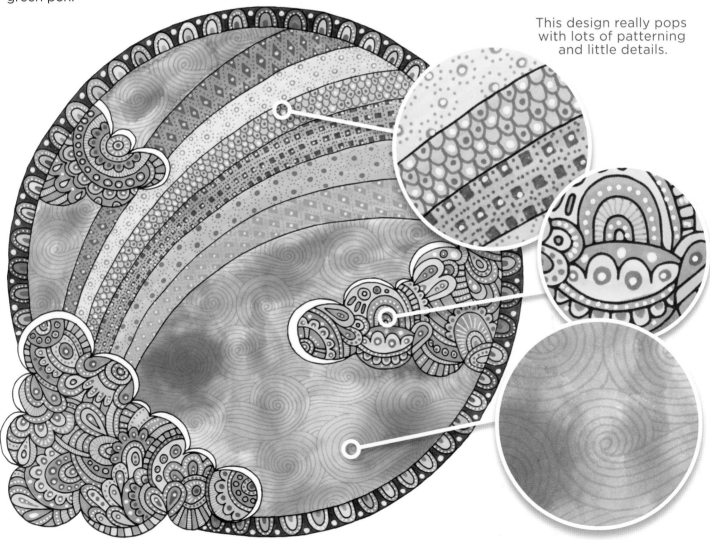

Coloring Supplies

I'm always asked about the mediums I use to color my illustrations. The answer would be really long if I listed every single thing, so here are a few of my favorites. Keep in mind that these are *my* favorites. When you color, you should use YOUR favorites!

Alcohol-based markers. I have many, and a variety of brands. My favorites have a brush nib—it's so versatile. A brush nib is perfect for tiny, tight corners, but is also able to cover a large, open space easily. I find I rarely get streaking, and if I do, it's usually because the ink is running low!

Fine-tip pens. Just like with markers, I have lots of different pens. I use them for my layers of detail work and for the itsy bitsy spots my markers can't get into.

Paint pens. These are wonderful! Because the ink is usually opaque, they stand out really well against a dark base color. I use extra fine point pens for their precision. Some paint pens are water based, so I can use a brush to blend the colors and create a cool watercolor effect.

Gel pens. I have a few, but I usually stick to white and neon colors that will stand out on top of dark base colors or other mediums.

  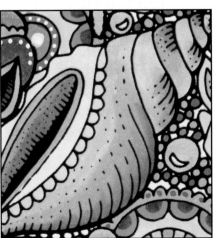

Hello Angel #1329 Island Princess: marker pens, fineliner pens, paint pens

Hello Angel #1330 Unibow Skies: marker pens, fineliner pens, paint pens

Hello Angel #1331 Catch and Release: marker pens, fineliner pens, paint pens

Hello Angel #1332 Deep Dive: watercolors, marker pens, fineliner pens, paint pens

 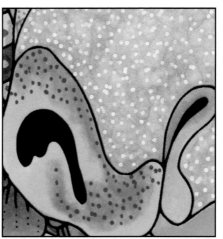 

Hello Angel #1333 Rare Beauty: watercolors, marker pens, fineliner pens, paint pens

Hello Angel #1334 Fantasy Cottage: watercolors, marker pens, fineliner pens, paint pens

Hello Angel #1335 Sensational Scales: watercolors, marker pens, fineliner pens, paint pens

Hello Angel #1336 Dreamicorn: watercolors, marker pens, fineliner pens, paint pens, colored pencils

Those who don't believe in magic will never find it.

—ROALD DAHL, *THE MINPINS*

Always be yourself,
unless you can be a unicorn.
Then always be a unicorn.

—UNKNOWN

In dreams we enter a world
that is entirely our own.

—HARRY POTTER AND THE PRISONER
OF AZKABAN

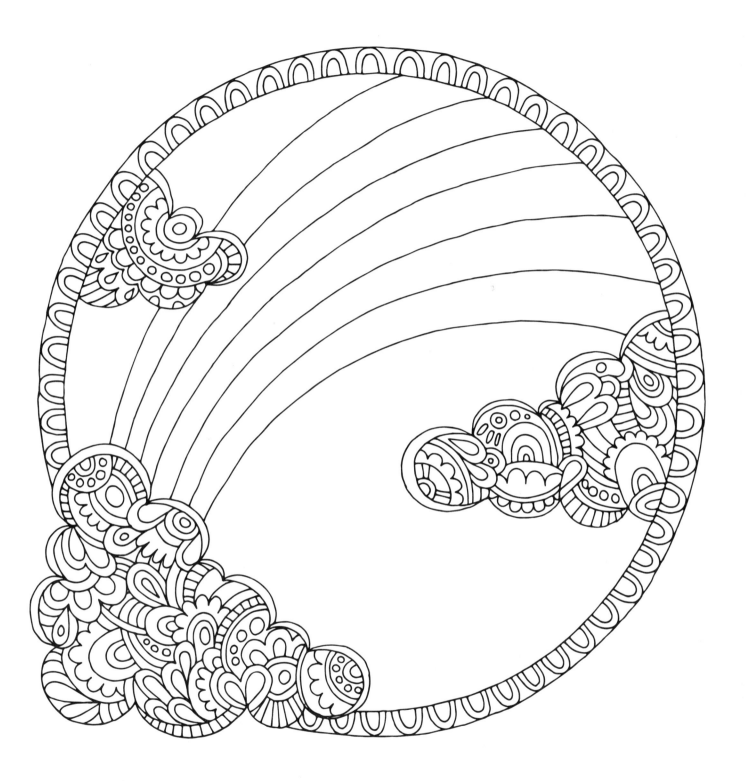

Be a rainbow in someone else's cloud.

—MAYA ANGELOU

By being yourself, you put something wonderful in the world that was not there before.

—EDWIN ELLIOT

Hello Angel #1325 Carnival Queen

When someone told me
that I live in a fantasyland,
I nearly fell off my unicorn.

—Unknown

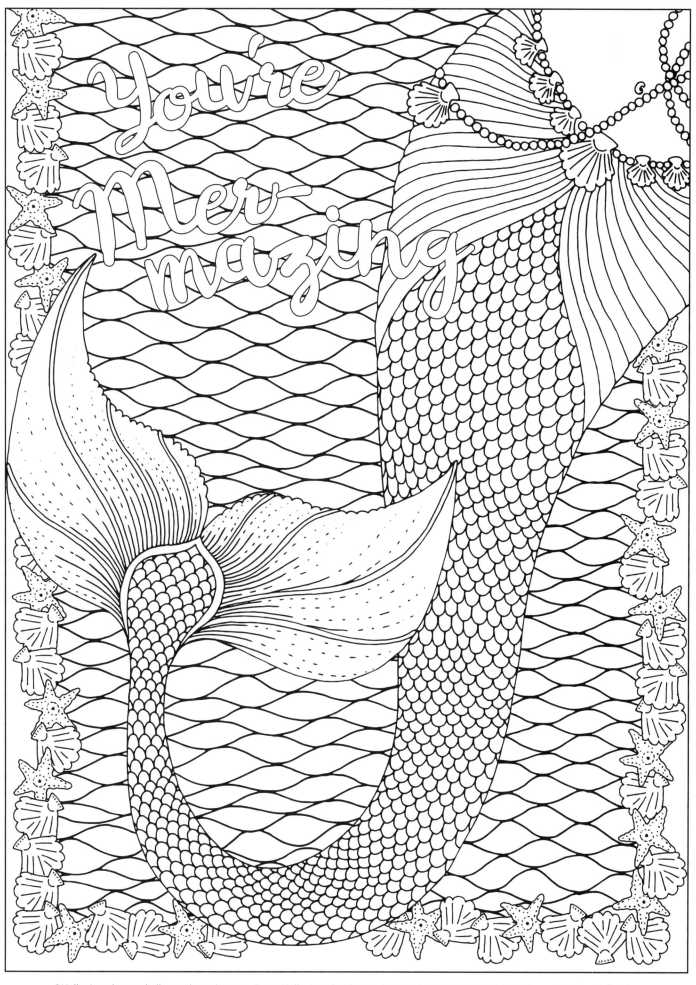

You're Mer-mazing

Who says that my dreams have
to stay just my dreams?

—ARIEL, *THE LITTLE MERMAID*

A rustle in the wind reminds
us that a fairy is near.

—UNKNOWN

With some basic shading techniques, maybe using deep purples and blues as in the example, you can give this island princess enchanting eyes.

It's impossible to make your eyes twinkle if you aren't feeling twinkly yourself.

—ROALD DAHL, *DANNY THE CHAMPION OF THE WORLD*

_____
_____
_____
_____
_____
_____
_____
_____
_____

Hello Angel #1329 Island Princess

Your unicorns (all eight of them) can be all the same color, or you can mix it up—either way they'll look happy flying among the rainbows!

It's going to be a rainbows
and unicorns kind of day.

—UNKNOWN

Hello Angel #1330 Unibow Skies

You can make a focal point of the fairy; try layering at least two hues
of whatever hair color you choose to create visual texture.

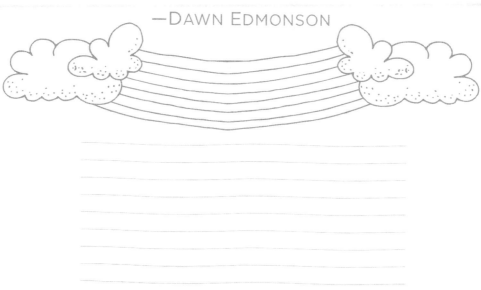

If you should catch a fairy
and place it in a jar,
Be sure to treat it kindly
and do not take it far—
This fairy is not for the keeping.
It has a home, you see.
The forest is a wonderful place
and fairies must live free.

—Dawn Edmonson

Hello Angel #1331 Catch and Release

Make your blue oceanic background feel like a tapestry
by washing out some of the dark color in places.

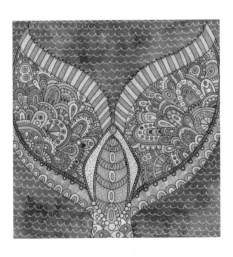

Mermaid Wisdom:
Get your tail to the beach.
See treasures in simple things.
Be calm in the storm.
Believe in magic!

—UNKNOWN

Hello Angel #1332 Deep Dive

The expression of this unicorn says business, but the glittering rainbow of its mane is all fun!

If I'm honest, I have to tell
you that I still read fairy tales
and I like them best of all.

—AUDREY HEPBURN

Hello Angel #1333 Rare Beauty

Who's home? Suggest a boisterous house party by shading
in silhouettes in the warmly glowing windows.

Some day you will be old enough
to start reading fairy tales again.

—C. S. LEWIS, *THE LION, THE WITCH
AND THE WARDROBE*

Hello Angel #1334 Fantasy Cottage

Even though this illustration comes with plenty of patterning already,
see how you can enhance it further by adding even more doodles.

Be a mermaid and make waves.

—Unknown

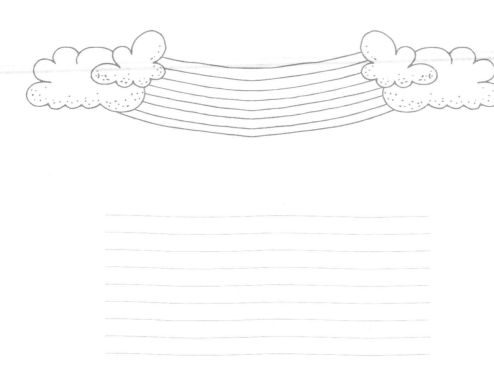

Hello Angel #1335 Sensational Scales

Add a touch of realism to this fantastical picture with some shading underneath the mane—your unicorn will look practically pettable!

Haven't you ever been in a fairy tale before?

—Peter S. Beagle, *The Last Unicorn*

Hello Angel #1336 Dreamicorn

When it rains on your parade,
look up rather than down.
Without the rain, there
would be no rainbow.

—G. K. CHESTERTON

A long time ago,
when the earth was still green,
there were more kinds of animals
than you've ever seen;
They'd run around free
while the earth was being born,
and the loveliest of all
was the unicorn.

—SHEL SILVERSTEIN, "THE UNICORN"

When it rains, look for rainbows.
When it's dark, look for stars.

—UNKNOWN

I must be a mermaid.
I have no fear of depths and
a great fear of shallow living.

—ANAÏS NIN, *THE FOUR-CHAMBERED HEART*

My soul is full of longing
for the secret of the sea,
and the heart of the great ocean
sends a thrilling pulse through me.

—HENRY WADSWORTH LONGFELLOW,
"THE SECRET OF THE SEA"

The universe is full of magical things patiently waiting for our wits to grow sharper.

—Eden Phillpotts

Everything you look at can become
a fairy tale and you can get a story
from everything you touch.

—HANS CHRISTIAN ANDERSEN

Imagination is the only weapon in the war against reality.

—LEWIS CARROLL, *ALICE'S ADVENTURES IN WONDERLAND*

_____
_____
_____
_____
_____
_____
_____
_____
_____
_____

Garden fairies come at dawn,
bless the flowers, then they're gone.

—UNKNOWN

Hello Angel #1345 Dance with Fairies

RIDE UNICORNS

Play with fairies,
ride a unicorn,
swim with mermaids,
chase rainbows.

—UNKNOWN

Someday we'll find it,
the rainbow connection
The lovers, the dreamers, and me.

—*THE MUPPET MOVIE*

SWIM WITH MERMAIDS

Dive in and explore
your heart's calling.

—UNKNOWN

_____

_____

_____

_____

_____

_____

_____

_____

If you really want to catch your dreams, you have to chase them.

—UNKNOWN

The difference between fairies
and you is that your wings are
hidden in your heart.

—UNKNOWN

_____

_____

_____

_____

_____

_____

_____

_____

Happiness is...
pretending to be a mermaid
in the swimming pool.

—Unknown

_____

_____

_____

_____

_____

_____

_____

_____

_____

Laughter is timeless, imagination
has no age, and dreams are forever.

—UNKNOWN

_____

_____

_____

_____

_____

_____

_____

_____

_____